{ BIBLE READING }

JOURNAL

NAVPRESS

NAVPRESS

Discipleship Inside Out®

NavPress is the publishing ministry of The Navigators, an international Christian organization and leader in personal spiritual development. NavPress is committed to helping people grow spiritually and enjoy lives of meaning and hope through personal and group resources that are biblically rooted, culturally relevant, and highly practical.

For a free catalog go to www.NavPress.com.

From 1981 to 2009, NavPress published *Discipleship Journal*, a magazine designed to provide timeless resources that helped people grow deeper in their relationship with Jesus Christ. *Discipleship Journal*'s Bible reading plans, published in the magazine each year, helped many people get into the Word; we hope they'll do the same for you.

© 2007 by *Discipleship Journal*®

A NavPress resource published by NavPress in alliance with Tyndale House Publishers, Inc., Carol Stream, Illinois, 60188

www.navpress.com

The Discipleship Journal Book-at-a-Time Bible Reading Plan used by permission of Mark Bogart and Peter Mayberry. © 2005 by *Discipleship Journal*.®

ISBN 978-1-60006-224-7

Visit the *Discipleship Journal*® magazine website at www.discipleshipjournal.com.

Cover Design by Adele Mulford
Cover Image by Ben Ng/Millennium Images UK

Printed in the United States of America.

20 19 18 17 16 15 14
10   9   8   7   6   5   4

INTRODUCTION

Nearly 30 years ago, a friend showed me how I could read through the Bible in a year. The plan she gave me was a lot like the one in this *Discipleship Journal Bible Reading Journal*: specific readings for each day with space to write about anything that caught my attention as I read.

I knew bits and pieces of the Bible at that point, but I had never read it from cover to cover. Doing so was life-transforming. Certain attitudes and actions underwent extreme makeovers. I acquired biblical wisdom to apply to daily challenges or to pass along when counseling a friend. When tough times hit, I found myself facing them with hope and grit. And when good times prevailed, I discovered a language for expressing my delight.

But most of all, I encountered God. The breadth of His character, His ways, and His redemptive purposes—as revealed in the grand span of Scripture—caused my heart to soar. Just as He was everywhere in the Bible, I began to see Him everywhere in my life. I had known about God all my life, but now I was gaining something more than knowledge: I was entering into an intimate, life-giving relationship with God.

The *Discipleship Journal Bible Reading Journal* is a way to share with you that experience of encountering God in the pages of Scripture. The *Journal* makes reading through the Bible flexible and doable for you. Here's how it works:

- You can start at any time (please don't think you must wait until January 1!) and in any portion of Scripture.

- We've provided two readings for each day. The first reading alternates Old and New Testament books, giving you three or four chapters a day. The second reading takes you through a chapter or so of the wisdom books or Isaiah each day.

- These readings are designed to lead you through the Bible in one year. But don't get too fixated on the one-year time frame. What really matters is getting acquainted with the entire Bible and glimpsing that big picture of who God is and what He is doing in the world. Take two years if you need to. Take three or more.

- Each month consists of only 25 readings. That means that if you are aiming for the one-year reading plan, you will have a few days each month to meditate more deeply on something that was significant to you in the past week or to catch up on missed readings.

- With each reading, we've included space for you to record highlights, insights, and questions from your reading.

- You'll also find, interspersed throughout this journal, some brief excerpts and quotes from 25 years of *Discipleship Journal* that will inspire you to keep reading and give you ideas for getting more of God's Word into your heart and mind and soul.

It's that simple. All that's left to say is, enjoy your reading!

—*Sue Kline*
Associate Publisher, Discipleship Journal

O LORD,

our Lord,

how majestic

is your name

in all

the earth!

Ps. 8:9

MONTH 1

DATE: _____

TODAY'S READING: Genesis 1-2, Psalm 1

MY THOUGHTS: _____

_____

_____

_____

_____

_____

_____

_____

_____

_____

_____

_____

_____

DATE: _____

TODAY'S READING: Genesis 3-5, Psalm 2

MY THOUGHTS: _____

_____

_____

_____

_____

_____

_____

_____

_____

_____

_____

_____

_____

DATE: ————————————

TODAY'S READING: Genesis 6-9, Psalm 3

MY THOUGHTS: ————————————

_____

_____

_____

_____

_____

_____

_____

_____

_____

_____

_____

_____

_____

DATE: ————————————

TODAY'S READING: Genesis 10-11, Psalm 4

MY THOUGHTS: ————————————

_____

_____

_____

_____

_____

_____

_____

_____

_____

_____

_____

_____

DATE: _____

TODAY'S READING: Genesis 12-14, Psalm 5

MY THOUGHTS: _____

_____

_____

_____

_____

_____

_____

_____

_____

_____

_____

_____

_____

_____

DATE: _____

TODAY'S READING: Genesis 15-17, Psalm 6

MY THOUGHTS: _____

_____

_____

_____

_____

_____

_____

_____

_____

_____

_____

_____

_____

_____

DATE: _____

MY THOUGHTS ON THIS WEEK'S READINGS: _____

_____

_____

_____

_____

_____

_____

_____

_____

_____

_____

_____

_____

_____

_____

_____

DATE: _____

TODAY'S READING: Genesis 18-20, Psalm 7

MY THOUGHTS: _____

_____

_____

_____

_____

_____

_____

_____

_____

_____

_____

_____

_____

DATE:_____

TODAY'S READING: Genesis 21-23, Psalm 8

MY THOUGHTS:_____

_____

_____

_____

_____

_____

_____

_____

_____

_____

_____

_____

_____

_____

DATE:_____

TODAY'S READING: Genesis 24-26, Psalm 9

MY THOUGHTS:_____

_____

_____

_____

_____

_____

_____

_____

_____

_____

_____

_____

_____

DATE: ———————————————

TODAY'S READING: Genesis 27-29, Psalm 10

MY THOUGHTS: ———————————————————————

_____

_____

_____

_____

_____

_____

_____

_____

_____

_____

_____

_____

DATE: ———————————————

TODAY'S READING: Genesis 30-32, Psalm 11

MY THOUGHTS: ———————————————————————

_____

_____

_____

_____

_____

_____

_____

_____

_____

_____

_____

DATE: _____

TODAY'S READING: Genesis 33–36, Psalm 12

MY THOUGHTS: _____

_____

_____

_____

_____

_____

_____

_____

_____

_____

_____

_____

_____

_____

DATE: _____

MY THOUGHTS ON THIS WEEK'S READINGS: _____

_____

_____

_____

_____

_____

_____

_____

_____

_____

_____

_____

_____

_____

_____

DATE: —————————————

TODAY'S READING: Genesis 37–39, Psalm 13

MY THOUGHTS: _____

_____

_____

_____

_____

_____

_____

_____

_____

_____

_____

_____

_____

_____

_____

DATE: —————————————

TODAY'S READING: Genesis 40–42, Psalm 14

MY THOUGHTS: _____

_____

_____

_____

_____

_____

_____

_____

_____

_____

_____

_____

_____

_____

DATE:_____

TODAY'S READING: Genesis 43–46, Psalm 15

MY THOUGHTS:_____

_____

_____

_____

_____

_____

_____

_____

_____

_____

_____

_____

_____

_____

_____

DATE:_____

TODAY'S READING: Genesis 47–50, Psalm 16

MY THOUGHTS:_____

_____

_____

_____

_____

_____

_____

_____

_____

_____

_____

_____

_____

_____

_____

DATE: ————————————

TODAY'S READING: Mark 1-3, Psalm 17

MY THOUGHTS: ————————————

_____

_____

_____

_____

_____

_____

_____

_____

_____

_____

_____

_____

_____

_____

DATE: ————————————

TODAY'S READING: Mark 4-6, Psalm 18:1-24

MY THOUGHTS: ————————————

_____

_____

_____

_____

_____

_____

_____

_____

_____

_____

_____

_____

_____

_____

DATE:_____

MY THOUGHTS ON THIS WEEK'S READINGS:_____

_____

_____

_____

_____

_____

_____

_____

_____

_____

_____

_____

_____

_____

DATE:_____

TODAY'S READING: Mark 7-9, Psalm 18:25-50

MY THOUGHTS:_____

_____

_____

_____

_____

_____

_____

_____

_____

_____

_____

_____

DATE: _____

TODAY'S READING: Mark 10-12, Psalm 19

MY THOUGHTS: _____

_____

_____

_____

_____

_____

_____

_____

_____

_____

_____

_____

_____

_____

DATE: _____

TODAY'S READING: Mark 13-16, Psalm 20

MY THOUGHTS: _____

_____

_____

_____

_____

_____

_____

_____

_____

_____

_____

_____

_____

DATE: _____

TODAY'S READING: Exodus 1–4, Psalm 21

MY THOUGHTS: _____

_____

_____

_____

_____

_____

_____

_____

_____

_____

_____

_____

_____

DATE: _____

TODAY'S READING: Exodus 5–8, Psalm 22:1–11

MY THOUGHTS: _____

_____

_____

_____

_____

_____

_____

_____

_____

_____

_____

_____

_____

_____

DATE: ———————————————

TODAY'S READING: Exodus 9-11, Psalm 22:12-31

MY THOUGHTS: ————————————————————

_____

_____

_____

_____

_____

_____

_____

_____

_____

_____

_____

_____

_____

DATE: ———————————————

TODAY'S READING: Exodus 12-14, Psalm 23

MY THOUGHTS: ————————————————————

_____

_____

_____

_____

_____

_____

_____

_____

_____

_____

_____

_____

_____

HOW TO GET THE MOST FROM YOUR BIBLE READING
by Robert Boardman

- Always pray before you read. Early in my Christian life I learned this prayer from Ps. 119:18: "Open my eyes that I may see wonderful things in your law." More than 50 years later I still pray this or other prayers for God's help and enlightenment.
- Read your Bible early in the morning, before breakfast if possible. The quiet of the dawn, when mind and heart can focus on God in His Word, is the best time of day for many. A motto I heard years ago still challenges me: "No Bible, No Breakfast."

   If for some reason this isn't feasible, pray for a better time of day. For many years I commuted one hour into the heart of Tokyo three or four times a week. I reserved the hour inbound each day for Bible reading only.
- If you commute by car, get the Bible on tape or CD in the version you use, and reserve blocks of time for Bible listening. But stay alert while you're driving!
- Mark important words or topics. (Use a pen with ink that won't soak through the pages.) For instance, you might mark the prominence God gives to His Word, or passages dealing with fear, the deity of Christ, or discipleship. Through many Old Testament books such as Ezekiel, Haggai, Zephaniah, and Jeremiah I have highlighted wherever God says, "I will" to show His determination and sovereignty to keep His promises. Think through carefully how you want to mark your Bible so you don't do it indiscriminately.
- Note carefully and mark sins that put Christians on the shelf. Are there sins for you especially to watch for and avoid, or impediments that you must set aside?
- As you read, ask yourself, *Do today's chapters give me new insights into the Lord Jesus Christ and His sinless life and dynamic ministry? Do I have any new thoughts about God?*
- Record your prayers, with the date and place, in the margins beside promises of God. Claim God's great and precious promises by faith, and then record answers when God fulfills them.
- Read expectantly and humbly. Believe God is going to meet with you and speak through His Holy Spirit in a special way. He longs to bless, lead, and draw you and make you a blessing to others.

—*Excerpted from "As You Read through the Bible"* (Discipleship Journal, *Issue 49*).

The fear
of the LORD
is the
beginning of
wisdom, and
knowledge
of the
Holy One is
understanding.

Prov. 9:10

MONTH 2

DATE:_____

TODAY'S READING: Exodus 15-17, Proverbs 1

MY THOUGHTS:_____

_____

_____

_____

_____

_____

_____

_____

_____

_____

_____

_____

_____

DATE:_____

TODAY'S READING: Exodus 18-20, Proverbs 2

MY THOUGHTS:_____

_____

_____

_____

_____

_____

_____

_____

_____

_____

_____

_____

_____

DATE: _____

TODAY'S READING: Exodus 21-24, Proverbs 3

MY THOUGHTS: _____

_____

_____

_____

_____

_____

_____

_____

_____

_____

_____

_____

_____

_____

DATE: _____

TODAY'S READING: Exodus 25-27, Proverbs 4

MY THOUGHTS: _____

_____

_____

_____

_____

_____

_____

_____

_____

_____

_____

_____

_____

_____

DATE:_____

TODAY'S READING: Exodus 28–31, Proverbs 5

MY THOUGHTS:_____

_____

_____

_____

_____

_____

_____

_____

_____

_____

_____

_____

_____

_____

_____

_____

DATE:_____

TODAY'S READING: Exodus 32–34, Proverbs 6

MY THOUGHTS:_____

_____

_____

_____

_____

_____

_____

_____

_____

_____

_____

_____

_____

_____

_____

_____

DATE: _____

MY THOUGHTS ON THIS WEEK'S READINGS: _____

_____

_____

_____

_____

_____

_____

_____

_____

_____

_____

_____

_____

_____

DATE: _____

TODAY'S READING: Exodus 35–37, Proverbs 7

MY THOUGHTS: _____

_____

_____

_____

_____

_____

_____

_____

_____

_____

_____

_____

_____

DATE: _____

TODAY'S READING: Exodus 38–40, Proverbs 8

MY THOUGHTS: _____

_____

_____

_____

_____

_____

_____

_____

_____

_____

_____

_____

_____

DATE: _____

TODAY'S READING: Acts 1-3, Proverbs 9

MY THOUGHTS: _____

_____

_____

_____

_____

_____

_____

_____

_____

_____

_____

_____

_____

DATE: ─────────────

TODAY'S READING: Acts 4–6, Proverbs 10:1-16

MY THOUGHTS: ───────────────────────────

_____

_____

_____

_____

_____

_____

_____

_____

_____

_____

_____

_____

_____

DATE: ─────────────

TODAY'S READING: Acts 7–9, Proverbs 10:17-32

MY THOUGHTS: ───────────────────────────

_____

_____

_____

_____

_____

_____

_____

_____

_____

_____

_____

_____

_____

DATE: _____

TODAY'S READING: Acts 10-12, Proverbs 11:1-15

MY THOUGHTS: _____

_____

_____

_____

_____

_____

_____

_____

_____

_____

_____

_____

_____

DATE: _____

MY THOUGHTS ON THIS WEEK'S READINGS: _____

_____

_____

_____

_____

_____

_____

_____

_____

_____

_____

_____

_____

DATE: _____

TODAY'S READING: Acts 13-15, Proverbs 11:16-31

MY THOUGHTS: _____

_____

_____

_____

_____

_____

_____

_____

_____

_____

_____

_____

_____

_____

_____

DATE: _____

TODAY'S READING: Acts 16-18, Proverbs 12:1-14

MY THOUGHTS: _____

_____

_____

_____

_____

_____

_____

_____

_____

_____

_____

_____

_____

_____

_____

DATE: _____

TODAY'S READING: Acts 19-21, Proverbs 12:15-28

MY THOUGHTS: _____

_____

_____

_____

_____

_____

_____

_____

_____

_____

_____

_____

_____

DATE: _____

TODAY'S READING: Acts 22-25, Proverbs 13:1-12

MY THOUGHTS: _____

_____

_____

_____

_____

_____

_____

_____

_____

_____

_____

_____

_____

DATE: —————————————

TODAY'S READING: Acts 26-28, Proverbs 13:13-25

MY THOUGHTS: ———————————————————————

_____

_____

_____

_____

_____

_____

_____

_____

_____

_____

_____

_____

_____

DATE: —————————————

TODAY'S READING: Leviticus 1-4, Proverbs 14:1-18

MY THOUGHTS: ———————————————————————

_____

_____

_____

_____

_____

_____

_____

_____

_____

_____

_____

_____

_____

DATE: _____

MY THOUGHTS ON THIS WEEK'S READINGS: _____

_____

_____

_____

_____

_____

_____

_____

_____

_____

_____

_____

_____

_____

DATE: _____

TODAY'S READING: Leviticus 5-8, Proverbs 14:19-35

MY THOUGHTS: _____

_____

_____

_____

_____

_____

_____

_____

_____

_____

_____

_____

_____

DATE: ————————————————

TODAY'S READING: Leviticus 9–11, Proverbs 15:1–17

MY THOUGHTS: ——————————————————————————————————————

_____

_____

_____

_____

_____

_____

_____

_____

_____

_____

_____

_____

DATE: ————————————————

TODAY'S READING: Leviticus 12–14, Proverbs 15:18–33

MY THOUGHTS: ——————————————————————————————————————

_____

_____

_____

_____

_____

_____

_____

_____

_____

_____

_____

_____

DATE: _____

TODAY'S READING: Leviticus 15–18, Proverbs 16:1-16

MY THOUGHTS: _____

_____

_____

_____

_____

_____

_____

_____

_____

_____

_____

_____

_____

_____

_____

DATE: _____

TODAY'S READING: Leviticus 19–21, Proverbs 16:17-33

MY THOUGHTS: _____

_____

_____

_____

_____

_____

_____

_____

_____

_____

_____

_____

_____

_____

_____

DATE: _____
TODAY'S READING: Leviticus 22-24, Proverbs 17:1-14
MY THOUGHTS: _____

_____
_____
_____
_____
_____
_____
_____
_____
_____
_____
_____
_____
_____
_____

DATE: _____
TODAY'S READING: Leviticus 25-27, Proverbs 17:15-28
MY THOUGHTS: _____

_____
_____
_____
_____
_____
_____
_____
_____
_____
_____
_____
_____
_____
_____

OLD TESTAMENT TREASURES
by Mathew Woodley

For Christians, the Old Testament finds its ultimate fulfillment in the New Testament. The Old Testament unashamedly points to a new covenant (Jer. 31:31). We are promised a new heart and a new king who places us in a new kingdom. Under His reign, we experience a deeper measure of grace and forgiveness.

But the Old Testament is still crucial to our journey as Christians. It teaches us about God, ourselves, and the relationship between ourselves and God. Yes, some parts are confusing. Some stories will perplex, anger, or bore you. But read it anyway. Study it. Wrestle with it. Pray it. Then pray it some more, listening for the voice of your Beloved.

Listen carefully, and you will find the story of your own heart—your jealousy, doubt, hatred, anguish, and longing. You will also find the story of your beauty, worth, love, joy, and passion.

Listen carefully, and you will hear the voice of the living God. The God who is a consuming fire (Heb. 12:29). The God who judges the nations. The God who asks everything from us. The God who knows you by name and seeks you out. The God who loves you with an everlasting love, who dances over you with joy (Jer. 31:3, Zeph. 3:17). The God who invites you—personally, passionately—to enter the greatest love story ever written.

—Excerpted from "Why Is the Old Testament So Weird?" (Discipleship Journal, Issue 124).

The LORD
your God
has chosen you
out of all the
peoples on
the face of
the earth to be
his people,
his treasured
possession.

Dt. 7:6

MONTH 3

DATE:_____

TODAY'S READING: Hebrews 1-3, Psalm 24

MY THOUGHTS:_____

_____

_____

_____

_____

_____

_____

_____

_____

_____

_____

_____

_____

_____

_____

_____

DATE:_____

TODAY'S READING: Hebrews 4-6, Psalm 25

MY THOUGHTS:_____

_____

_____

_____

_____

_____

_____

_____

_____

_____

_____

_____

_____

_____

DATE: ———————————

TODAY'S READING: Hebrews 7–10, Psalm 26

MY THOUGHTS: ————————————————————————

_____

_____

_____

_____

_____

_____

_____

_____

_____

_____

_____

_____

DATE: ———————————

TODAY'S READING: Hebrews 11–13, Psalm 27

MY THOUGHTS: ————————————————————————

_____

_____

_____

_____

_____

_____

_____

_____

_____

_____

_____

_____

DATE: _____

TODAY'S READING: Numbers 1–3, Psalm 28

MY THOUGHTS: _____

_____

_____

_____

_____

_____

_____

_____

_____

_____

_____

_____

_____

_____

DATE: _____

TODAY'S READING: Numbers 4–7, Psalm 29

MY THOUGHTS: _____

_____

_____

_____

_____

_____

_____

_____

_____

_____

_____

_____

_____

DATE: _____

MY THOUGHTS ON THIS WEEK'S READINGS: _____

_____
_____
_____
_____
_____
_____
_____
_____
_____
_____
_____
_____
_____
_____

DATE: _____

TODAY'S READING: Numbers 8-10, Psalm 30

MY THOUGHTS: _____

_____
_____
_____
_____
_____
_____
_____
_____
_____
_____
_____
_____
_____

DATE: _____

TODAY'S READING: Numbers 11-14, Psalm 31

MY THOUGHTS: _____

_____

_____

_____

_____

_____

_____

_____

_____

_____

_____

_____

_____

DATE: _____

TODAY'S READING: Numbers 15-17, Psalm 32

MY THOUGHTS: _____

_____

_____

_____

_____

_____

_____

_____

_____

_____

_____

_____

_____

DATE: _____

TODAY'S READING: Numbers 18–21, Psalm 33

MY THOUGHTS: _____

_____

_____

_____

_____

_____

_____

_____

_____

_____

_____

_____

_____

DATE: _____

TODAY'S READING: Numbers 22–24, Psalm 34

MY THOUGHTS: _____

_____

_____

_____

_____

_____

_____

_____

_____

_____

_____

_____

_____

DATE: _____

TODAY'S READING: Numbers 25-27, Psalm 35

MY THOUGHTS: _____

_____

_____

_____

_____

_____

_____

_____

_____

_____

_____

_____

_____

_____

_____

DATE: _____

MY THOUGHTS ON THIS WEEK'S READINGS: _____

_____

_____

_____

_____

_____

_____

_____

_____

_____

_____

_____

_____

_____

DATE: —————————————

TODAY'S READING: Numbers 28-30, Psalm 36

MY THOUGHTS: ——————————————————————

————————————————————————————————
————————————————————————————————
————————————————————————————————
————————————————————————————————
————————————————————————————————
————————————————————————————————
————————————————————————————————
————————————————————————————————
————————————————————————————————
————————————————————————————————
————————————————————————————————
————————————————————————————————
————————————————————————————————

DATE: —————————————

TODAY'S READING: Numbers 31-33, Psalm 37:1-22

MY THOUGHTS: ——————————————————————

————————————————————————————————
————————————————————————————————
————————————————————————————————
————————————————————————————————
————————————————————————————————
————————————————————————————————
————————————————————————————————
————————————————————————————————
————————————————————————————————
————————————————————————————————
————————————————————————————————
————————————————————————————————
————————————————————————————————

DATE:_____

TODAY'S READING: Numbers 34-36, Psalm 37:23-40

MY THOUGHTS:_____

_____

_____

_____

_____

_____

_____

_____

_____

_____

_____

_____

_____

_____

DATE:_____

TODAY'S READING: Galatians 1-3, Psalm 38

MY THOUGHTS:_____

_____

_____

_____

_____

_____

_____

_____

_____

_____

_____

_____

_____

DATE: —————————————————

TODAY'S READING: Galatians 4–6, Psalm 39

MY THOUGHTS: ————————————————————————

_____

_____

_____

_____

_____

_____

_____

_____

_____

_____

_____

_____

_____

DATE: —————————————————

TODAY'S READING: Deuteronomy 1–4, Psalm 40

MY THOUGHTS: ————————————————————————

_____

_____

_____

_____

_____

_____

_____

_____

_____

_____

_____

_____

DATE:_____

MY THOUGHTS ON THIS WEEK'S READINGS:_____

_____

_____

_____

_____

_____

_____

_____

_____

_____

_____

_____

_____

DATE:_____

TODAY'S READING: Deuteronomy 5-7, Psalm 41

MY THOUGHTS:_____

_____

_____

_____

_____

_____

_____

_____

_____

_____

_____

_____

DATE: ———————————————

TODAY'S READING: Deuteronomy 8-10, Psalm 42

MY THOUGHTS: ————————————————————————————

_____

_____

_____

_____

_____

_____

_____

_____

_____

_____

_____

_____

_____

DATE: ———————————————

TODAY'S READING: Deuteronomy 11-13, Psalm 43

MY THOUGHTS: ————————————————————————————

_____

_____

_____

_____

_____

_____

_____

_____

_____

_____

_____

_____

DATE: _____

TODAY'S READING: Deuteronomy 14-16, Psalm 44

MY THOUGHTS: _____

_____

_____

_____

_____

_____

_____

_____

_____

_____

_____

_____

_____

DATE: _____

TODAY'S READING: Deuteronomy 17-19, Psalm 45

MY THOUGHTS: _____

_____

_____

_____

_____

_____

_____

_____

_____

_____

_____

_____

_____

DATE: ——————————————

TODAY'S READING: Deuteronomy 20-22, Psalm 46

MY THOUGHTS: ——————————————————————————————————

_____

_____

_____

_____

_____

_____

_____

_____

_____

_____

_____

DATE: ——————————————

TODAY'S READING: Deuteronomy 23-26, Psalm 47

MY THOUGHTS: ——————————————————————————————————

_____

_____

_____

_____

_____

_____

_____

_____

_____

_____

_____

T he Bible does not thrill, the Bible nourishes. Give time
   to the reading of the Bible and the recreating effect is
as real as that of fresh air physically.

—Oswald Chambers, Disciples Indeed

E very person in the world has 24 hours a day. The rich
   have no more, the poor have no less. Generally, these
24 hours are ours to use at our discretion, and we make
time for the things we most want to do or that we think
are the most important. We do them by choice, and not
because someone forces us.

The question that continually prods me is, How much
do I want to go deeper into God's Word and in knowing
Him intimately, and what am I willing to give up in order
to do it?

—Warren Myers, excerpted from "Digging Deeper in God's Word"
(Discipleship Journal, *Issue 6*)

The secret
things belong
to the LORD
our God,
but the things
revealed belong
to us and to our
children forever,
that we may
follow all the
words of this law.

Dt. 29:29

MONTH 4

DATE: _____

TODAY'S READING: Deuteronomy 27-30, Psalm 48

MY THOUGHTS: _____

DATE: _____

TODAY'S READING: Deuteronomy 31-34, Psalm 49

MY THOUGHTS: _____

DATE: ———————————

TODAY'S READING: James 1-2, Psalm 50

MY THOUGHTS: ———————————

_____

_____

_____

_____

_____

_____

_____

_____

_____

_____

_____

_____

_____

DATE: ———————————

TODAY'S READING: James 3-5, Psalm 51

MY THOUGHTS: ———————————

_____

_____

_____

_____

_____

_____

_____

_____

_____

_____

_____

_____

_____

DATE: _____

TODAY'S READING: Joshua 1-3, Psalm 52

MY THOUGHTS: _____

_____

_____

_____

_____

_____

_____

_____

_____

_____

_____

_____

_____

DATE: _____

TODAY'S READING: Joshua 4-6, Psalm 53

MY THOUGHTS: _____

_____

_____

_____

_____

_____

_____

_____

_____

_____

_____

_____

_____

DATE: _____

MY THOUGHTS ON THIS WEEK'S READINGS: _____

_____

_____

_____

_____

_____

_____

_____

_____

_____

_____

_____

_____

_____

_____

DATE: _____

TODAY'S READING: Joshua 7-9, Psalm 54

MY THOUGHTS: _____

_____

_____

_____

_____

_____

_____

_____

_____

_____

_____

_____

_____

DATE: _____

TODAY'S READING: Joshua 10–12, Psalm 55

MY THOUGHTS: _____

_____

_____

_____

_____

_____

_____

_____

_____

_____

_____

_____

_____

_____

DATE: _____

TODAY'S READING: Joshua 13–15, Psalm 56

MY THOUGHTS: _____

_____

_____

_____

_____

_____

_____

_____

_____

_____

_____

_____

_____

_____

DATE: ———————————

TODAY'S READING: Joshua 16-18, Psalm 57

MY THOUGHTS: ———————————————————————

———————————————————————————————————————

———————————————————————————————————————

———————————————————————————————————————

———————————————————————————————————————

———————————————————————————————————————

———————————————————————————————————————

———————————————————————————————————————

———————————————————————————————————————

———————————————————————————————————————

———————————————————————————————————————

———————————————————————————————————————

———————————————————————————————————————

DATE: ———————————

TODAY'S READING: Joshua 19-21, Psalm 58

MY THOUGHTS: ———————————————————————

———————————————————————————————————————

———————————————————————————————————————

———————————————————————————————————————

———————————————————————————————————————

———————————————————————————————————————

———————————————————————————————————————

———————————————————————————————————————

———————————————————————————————————————

———————————————————————————————————————

———————————————————————————————————————

———————————————————————————————————————

———————————————————————————————————————

DATE: _____

TODAY'S READING: Joshua 22–24, Psalm 59

MY THOUGHTS: _____

_____

_____

_____

_____

_____

_____

_____

_____

_____

_____

_____

_____

DATE: _____

MY THOUGHTS ON THIS WEEK'S READINGS: _____

_____

_____

_____

_____

_____

_____

_____

_____

_____

_____

_____

_____

_____

DATE: —————————————————
TODAY'S READING: Matthew 1-4, Psalm 60
MY THOUGHTS: ————————————————————————————————

———
———
———
———
———
———
———
———
———
———
———
———

DATE: —————————————————
TODAY'S READING: Matthew 5-7, Psalm 61
MY THOUGHTS: ————————————————————————————————

———
———
———
———
———
———
———
———
———
———
———
———

DATE:_____

TODAY'S READING: Matthew 8-10, Psalm 62

MY THOUGHTS:_____

_____

_____

_____

_____

_____

_____

_____

_____

_____

_____

_____

_____

DATE:_____

TODAY'S READING: Matthew 11-13, Psalm 63

MY THOUGHTS:_____

_____

_____

_____

_____

_____

_____

_____

_____

_____

_____

_____

DATE: _____

TODAY'S READING: Matthew 14-16, Psalm 64

MY THOUGHTS: _____

_____

_____

_____

_____

_____

_____

_____

_____

_____

_____

_____

_____

_____

DATE: _____

TODAY'S READING: Matthew 17-19, Psalm 65

MY THOUGHTS: _____

_____

_____

_____

_____

_____

_____

_____

_____

_____

_____

_____

_____

_____

DATE: _____

MY THOUGHTS ON THIS WEEK'S READINGS: _____

_____

_____

_____

_____

_____

_____

_____

_____

_____

_____

_____

_____

_____

DATE: _____

TODAY'S READING: Matthew 20-22, Psalm 66

MY THOUGHTS: _____

_____

_____

_____

_____

_____

_____

_____

_____

_____

_____

_____

_____

DATE: ───────────────
TODAY'S READING: Matthew 23-25, Psalm 67
MY THOUGHTS: ───────────────────────────────

_____
_____
_____
_____
_____
_____
_____
_____
_____
_____
_____
_____
_____

DATE: ───────────────
TODAY'S READING: Matthew 26-28, Psalm 68
MY THOUGHTS: ───────────────────────────────

_____
_____
_____
_____
_____
_____
_____
_____
_____
_____
_____
_____
_____

DATE: _____

TODAY'S READING: Judges 1-3, Psalm 69:1-18

MY THOUGHTS: _____

_____

_____

_____

_____

_____

_____

_____

_____

_____

_____

_____

_____

DATE: _____

TODAY'S READING: Judges 4-6, Psalm 69:19-36

MY THOUGHTS: _____

_____

_____

_____

_____

_____

_____

_____

_____

_____

_____

_____

_____

DATE: —————————————————

TODAY'S READING: Judges 7–9, Psalm 70

MY THOUGHTS: ——————————————————————————

———————————————————————————————————————

———————————————————————————————————————

———————————————————————————————————————

———————————————————————————————————————

———————————————————————————————————————

———————————————————————————————————————

———————————————————————————————————————

———————————————————————————————————————

———————————————————————————————————————

———————————————————————————————————————

———————————————————————————————————————

———————————————————————————————————————

———————————————————————————————————————

DATE: —————————————————

TODAY'S READING: Judges 10–12, Psalm 71

MY THOUGHTS: ——————————————————————————

———————————————————————————————————————

———————————————————————————————————————

———————————————————————————————————————

———————————————————————————————————————

———————————————————————————————————————

———————————————————————————————————————

———————————————————————————————————————

———————————————————————————————————————

———————————————————————————————————————

———————————————————————————————————————

———————————————————————————————————————

———————————————————————————————————————

WHY READ THE BIBLE DAILY?

by Robert Boardman

- It gives us a bird's-eye view of Scripture. Detailed Bible study is like mining for truth far beneath the earth's surface. We need that, but we also need the counter-balance of the broad, overall sweep that we get only by daily reading. Studying one portion yields helpful details, but reading by volume with a daily goal in mind gives a better overall perspective on the whole of Scripture.
- It helps prevent doctrinal tangents and sidetracks. False teachings can be difficult to discern. Almost all were formed when someone put all the emphasis on a few passages of Scripture taken out of context.
- It can keep us from majoring on the minors. Doctrinal issues that wrongly divide believers can be kept in perspective by reviewing the broad issues and events. Familiarity with the whole Word of God by constant and repeated reading helps us recognize when Scripture is being used out of context.
- It helps us refamiliarize ourselves with God's truth. As I read daily, I review my previous markings and notes in the margin of my Bible. Not to review every year means the possible loss of important truths, knowledge, and vital personal applications as well as specific direction for life and ministry.
- It makes difficult passages clear over time. A well-worn footpath through such difficult books as Revelation, parts of Daniel, and Haggai will make those rugged mountains increasingly familiar and understandable.
- It gives you a moral bath in spiritual truth. Daily Bible reading transports us from the secular, the physical, the cares of the day, to the heart of the living God, speaking to our inner being through His cleansing Word. How easy it is amid daily routines and relationships to develop unclean thoughts or to be offended by an unloving, harsh, thoughtless word! Only God's Word, washing us daily, can restore peace of mind and remove the resentment that naturally builds up. "Great peace have they who love your law, and nothing can make them stumble" (Ps. 119:165).

—Excerpted from "The Neglected Exercise" (Discipleship Journal, Issue 49).

O Sovereign
LORD, you are
God! Your words
are trustworthy,
and you have
promised these
good things to
your servant.

2 Sam. 7:28

MONTH 5

DATE: _____

TODAY'S READING: Judges 13–15, Proverbs 18

MY THOUGHTS: _____

_____

_____

_____

_____

_____

_____

_____

_____

_____

_____

_____

_____

DATE: _____

TODAY'S READING: Judges 16–18, Proverbs 19:1-14

MY THOUGHTS: _____

_____

_____

_____

_____

_____

_____

_____

_____

_____

_____

_____

_____

DATE: ──────────────

TODAY'S READING: Judges 19-21, Proverbs 19:15-29

MY THOUGHTS: ──────────────────────────

──────────────────────────────────────
──────────────────────────────────────
──────────────────────────────────────
──────────────────────────────────────
──────────────────────────────────────
──────────────────────────────────────
──────────────────────────────────────
──────────────────────────────────────
──────────────────────────────────────
──────────────────────────────────────
──────────────────────────────────────
──────────────────────────────────────

DATE: ──────────────

TODAY'S READING: Romans 1-3, Proverbs 20:1-15

MY THOUGHTS: ──────────────────────────

──────────────────────────────────────
──────────────────────────────────────
──────────────────────────────────────
──────────────────────────────────────
──────────────────────────────────────
──────────────────────────────────────
──────────────────────────────────────
──────────────────────────────────────
──────────────────────────────────────
──────────────────────────────────────
──────────────────────────────────────
──────────────────────────────────────

DATE: _____

TODAY'S READING: Romans 4-5, Proverbs 20:16-30

MY THOUGHTS: _____

_____

_____

_____

_____

_____

_____

_____

_____

_____

_____

_____

_____

_____

_____

DATE: _____

TODAY'S READING: Romans 6-8, Proverbs 21:1-16

MY THOUGHTS: _____

_____

_____

_____

_____

_____

_____

_____

_____

_____

_____

_____

_____

_____

_____

DATE: _____

MY THOUGHTS ON THIS WEEK'S READINGS: _____

_____

_____

_____

_____

_____

_____

_____

_____

_____

_____

_____

_____

_____

_____

DATE: _____

TODAY'S READING: Romans 9-11, Proverbs 21:17-31

MY THOUGHTS: _____

_____

_____

_____

_____

_____

_____

_____

_____

_____

_____

_____

_____

DATE:_____

TODAY'S READING: Romans 12-13, Proverbs 22:1-16

MY THOUGHTS:_____

_____

_____

_____

_____

_____

_____

_____

_____

_____

_____

_____

_____

_____

_____

DATE:_____

TODAY'S READING: Romans 14-16, Proverbs 22:17-29

MY THOUGHTS:_____

_____

_____

_____

_____

_____

_____

_____

_____

_____

_____

_____

_____

_____

_____

_____

DATE: _____

TODAY'S READING: Ruth, Proverbs 23:1-18

MY THOUGHTS: _____

_____

_____

_____

_____

_____

_____

_____

_____

_____

_____

DATE: _____

TODAY'S READING: Ephesians 1-3, Proverbs 23:19-35

MY THOUGHTS: _____

_____

_____

_____

_____

_____

_____

_____

_____

_____

_____

DATE:_____

TODAY'S READING: Ephesian 4-6, Proverbs 24:1-22

MY THOUGHTS:_____

_____

_____

_____

_____

_____

_____

_____

_____

_____

_____

_____

_____

DATE:_____

MY THOUGHTS ON THIS WEEK'S READINGS:_____

_____

_____

_____

_____

_____

_____

_____

_____

_____

_____

_____

_____

_____

DATE: _____

TODAY'S READING: 1 Samuel 1-3, Proverbs 24:23-34

MY THOUGHTS: _____

_____

_____

_____

_____

_____

_____

_____

_____

_____

_____

_____

_____

_____

DATE: _____

TODAY'S READING: 1 Samuel 4-6, Proverbs 25:1-14

MY THOUGHTS: _____

_____

_____

_____

_____

_____

_____

_____

_____

_____

_____

_____

_____

DATE:_____

TODAY'S READING: 1 Samuel 7-9, Proverbs 25:15-28

MY THOUGHTS:_____

_____

_____

_____

_____

_____

_____

_____

_____

_____

_____

_____

_____

DATE:_____

TODAY'S READING: 1 Samuel 10-12, Proverbs 26:1-16

MY THOUGHTS:_____

_____

_____

_____

_____

_____

_____

_____

_____

_____

_____

_____

_____

DATE: _____

TODAY'S READING: 1 Samuel 13-15, Proverbs 26:17-28

MY THOUGHTS: _____

_____

_____

_____

_____

_____

_____

_____

_____

_____

_____

_____

_____

_____

DATE: _____

TODAY'S READING: 1 Samuel 16-19, Proverbs 27:1-14

MY THOUGHTS: _____

_____

_____

_____

_____

_____

_____

_____

_____

_____

_____

_____

_____

_____

DATE:_____

MY THOUGHTS ON THIS WEEK'S READINGS:_____

_____

_____

_____

_____

_____

_____

_____

_____

_____

_____

_____

_____

_____

_____

DATE:_____

TODAY'S READING: 1 Samuel 20-22, Proverbs 27:15-27

MY THOUGHTS:_____

_____

_____

_____

_____

_____

_____

_____

_____

_____

_____

_____

_____

DATE: _____

TODAY'S READING: 1 Samuel 23-25, Proverbs 28:1-14

MY THOUGHTS: _____

_____

_____

_____

_____

_____

_____

_____

_____

_____

_____

_____

DATE: _____

TODAY'S READING: 1 Samuel 26-28, Proverbs 28:15-28

MY THOUGHTS: _____

_____

_____

_____

_____

_____

_____

_____

_____

_____

_____

_____

DATE: _____

TODAY'S READING: 1 Samuel 29-31, Proverbs 29:1-14

MY THOUGHTS: _____

_____

_____

_____

_____

_____

_____

_____

_____

_____

_____

_____

_____

DATE: _____

TODAY'S READING: Philippians, Proverbs 29:15-27

MY THOUGHTS: _____

_____

_____

_____

_____

_____

_____

_____

_____

_____

_____

_____

_____

_____

DATE: ———————————————

TODAY'S READING: 2 Samuel 1-3, Proverbs 30

MY THOUGHTS: ———————————————————————

_____

_____

_____

_____

_____

_____

_____

_____

_____

_____

_____

_____

_____

DATE: ———————————————

TODAY'S READING: 2 Samuel 4-7, Proverbs 31

MY THOUGHTS: ———————————————————————

_____

_____

_____

_____

_____

_____

_____

_____

_____

_____

_____

_____

Lord, you have searched me and you know me.
thoughts from afar. You discern my going out
thoughts from afar. You discern my going out

MY JOB AS CLAY
by Sue Kline

"**I** love reading my old journals and seeing how marvelously God has worked in my life!" the speaker enthused.

I slumped in my chair and grumbled inwardly: *Ha! The last time I reread my old journals, it made me feel as if I'd made no progress at all!*

The process of lifelong spiritual growth—of being shaped into the image of Christ—is much too slow and laborious for my tastes. God seems to be taking an inordinate amount of time turning me into the person I think I should be.

My response to His perceived pokiness has been to take matters into my own hands—to try harder with more Bible study, longer quiet times, increased serving at church. Which makes me wonder: How many of us have quit growing spiritually simply because we are worn out?

And in our fatigue, how many of us have assumed that God is worn out too? That this shaper of our lives, this divine Potter, is as discouraged with us as we are with ourselves? One of these days, I half believe, He's going to step back from His potter's wheel, shake His head sadly, and write me off as an intractable lump of clay.

But the real Potter—not the one of my warped imagination—says to me, "Be patient. My hands are always on you. You may not be able to discern what you are becoming; it may even seem to you as if I am improvising from one day to the next. But I know exactly what you will one day look like, and My hands will not leave you until you are perfect."

My spiritual growth is based not on my fever-pitched performance but on the true nature of my Potter: His mercy, power, love, grace, faithfulness . . . the list is endless. I will have patience with the process of growing only to the extent that I believe He holds my frustrations, my fears, and also my delights close to His Father-heart . . . and is acting in my life with wisdom and power whether it appears so or not.

My job as clay is to submit to my Potter's touch—to stay close to Him, to yield to the promptings of His hands in ready obedience, and to relax, knowing that "he who began a good work in [me] will carry it on to completion" (Phil. 1:6). He will not give up on me! And you know what else? He only creates masterpieces.

—*Excerpted from "Pottery Training"* (Discipleship Journal, *Issue 118).*

As for God,

his way is

perfect;

the word of

the LORD

is flawless.

2 Sam. 22:31

MONTH 6

DATE: _____

TODAY'S READING: 2 Samuel 8-10, Psalm 72

MY THOUGHTS: _____

_____

_____

_____

_____

_____

_____

_____

_____

_____

_____

_____

_____

_____

DATE: _____

TODAY'S READING: 2 Samuel 11-13, Psalm 73

MY THOUGHTS: _____

_____

_____

_____

_____

_____

_____

_____

_____

_____

_____

_____

_____

_____

DATE: ——————————————

TODAY'S READING: 2 Samuel 14-17, Psalm 74

MY THOUGHTS: ————————————————————————————

_____

_____

_____

_____

_____

_____

_____

_____

_____

_____

_____

DATE: ——————————————

TODAY'S READING: 2 Samuel 18-20, Psalm 75

MY THOUGHTS: ————————————————————————————

_____

_____

_____

_____

_____

_____

_____

_____

_____

_____

_____

DATE: _____

TODAY'S READING: 2 Samuel 21-24, Psalm 76

MY THOUGHTS: _____

_____
_____
_____
_____
_____
_____
_____
_____
_____
_____
_____
_____
_____

DATE: _____

TODAY'S READING: Colossians, Psalm 77

MY THOUGHTS: _____

_____
_____
_____
_____
_____
_____
_____
_____
_____
_____
_____
_____
_____

DATE: _____

MY THOUGHTS ON THIS WEEK'S READINGS: _____

_____
_____
_____
_____
_____
_____
_____
_____
_____
_____
_____
_____

DATE: _____

TODAY'S READING: 1 Kings 1-3, Psalm 78:1-39

MY THOUGHTS: _____

_____
_____
_____
_____
_____
_____
_____
_____
_____
_____
_____

DATE: _____

TODAY'S READING: 1 Kings 4-6, Psalm 78:40-72

MY THOUGHTS: _____

_____

_____

_____

_____

_____

_____

_____

_____

_____

_____

_____

_____

_____

DATE: _____

TODAY'S READING: 1 Kings 7-9, Psalm 79

MY THOUGHTS: _____

_____

_____

_____

_____

_____

_____

_____

_____

_____

_____

_____

_____

_____

DATE: _____

TODAY'S READING: 1 Kings 10-12, Psalm 80

MY THOUGHTS: _____

_____

_____

_____

_____

_____

_____

_____

_____

_____

_____

_____

_____

_____

DATE: _____

TODAY'S READING: 1 Kings 13-15, Psalm 81

MY THOUGHTS: _____

_____

_____

_____

_____

_____

_____

_____

_____

_____

_____

_____

_____

_____

DATE: _____

TODAY'S READING: 1 Kings 16-19, Psalm 82

MY THOUGHTS: _____

_____

_____

_____

_____

_____

_____

_____

_____

_____

_____

_____

_____

_____

DATE: _____

MY THOUGHTS ON THIS WEEK'S READINGS: _____

_____

_____

_____

_____

_____

_____

_____

_____

_____

_____

_____

_____

_____

_____

DATE: _____

TODAY'S READING: 1 Kings 20-22, Psalm 83

MY THOUGHTS: _____

_____

_____

_____

_____

_____

_____

_____

_____

_____

_____

_____

DATE: _____

TODAY'S READING: Jonah, Psalm 84

MY THOUGHTS: _____

_____

_____

_____

_____

_____

_____

_____

_____

_____

_____

_____

DATE: _____

TODAY'S READING: Philemon, Psalm 85

MY THOUGHTS: _____

_____

_____

_____

_____

_____

_____

_____

_____

_____

_____

_____

_____

_____

DATE: _____

TODAY'S READING: 2 Kings 1-4, Psalm 86

MY THOUGHTS: _____

_____

_____

_____

_____

_____

_____

_____

_____

_____

_____

_____

_____

_____

DATE: ───────────────
TODAY'S READING: 2 Kings 5-7, Psalm 87
MY THOUGHTS: ─────────────────────────────────────

_____
_____
_____
_____
_____
_____
_____
_____
_____
_____
_____
_____
_____

DATE: ───────────────
TODAY'S READING: 2 Kings 8-11, Psalm 88
MY THOUGHTS: ─────────────────────────────────────

_____
_____
_____
_____
_____
_____
_____
_____
_____
_____
_____
_____

DATE: _____

MY THOUGHTS ON THIS WEEK'S READINGS: _____

_____

_____

_____

_____

_____

_____

_____

_____

_____

_____

_____

_____

_____

_____

DATE: _____

TODAY'S READING: 2 Kings 12-14, Psalm 89:1-18

MY THOUGHTS: _____

_____

_____

_____

_____

_____

_____

_____

_____

_____

_____

_____

_____

DATE: ————————————

TODAY'S READING: 2 Kings 15–18, Psalm 89:19-52

MY THOUGHTS: ————————————————————

_____

_____

_____

_____

_____

_____

_____

_____

_____

_____

_____

_____

_____

DATE: ————————————

TODAY'S READING: 2 Kings 19-21, Psalm 90

MY THOUGHTS: ————————————————————

_____

_____

_____

_____

_____

_____

_____

_____

_____

_____

_____

_____

_____

DATE: _____

TODAY'S READING: 2 Kings 22–25, Psalm 91

MY THOUGHTS: _____

_____

_____

_____

_____

_____

_____

_____

_____

_____

_____

_____

_____

DATE: _____

TODAY'S READING: Luke 1–3, Psalm 92

MY THOUGHTS: _____

_____

_____

_____

_____

_____

_____

_____

_____

_____

_____

_____

_____

DATE: _____

TODAY'S READING: Luke 4–6, Psalm 93

MY THOUGHTS: _____

_____

_____

_____

_____

_____

_____

_____

_____

_____

_____

_____

_____

_____

DATE: _____

TODAY'S READING: Luke 7–9, Psalm 94

MY THOUGHTS: _____

_____

_____

_____

_____

_____

_____

_____

_____

_____

_____

_____

_____

_____

We should read the Scripture prayerfully, never supposing that we are clever enough or wise enough to understand God's Word by our own wisdom. In all our reading of the Scriptures let us seek carefully to have the help of the Holy Spirit; let us ask for Jesus' sake that He will enlighten us. He is willing to do it.

—*George Müller,* Spiritual Secrets of George Müller

QUESTIONS TO ASK
OF A BIBLE PASSAGE
- Is there an example for me to follow?
- Is there a command for me to obey?
- Is there an error for me to avoid?
- Is there a sin for me to forsake?
- Is there a promise for me to claim?
- Is there a new insight into God's character?

Sing to
the LORD,
a new song;
sing to the
LORD,
all the earth.

Ps. 96:1

MONTH 7

DATE:_____

TODAY'S READING: Luke 10–12, Ecclesiastes 1

MY THOUGHTS:_____

_____

_____

_____

_____

_____

_____

_____

_____

_____

_____

_____

_____

_____

DATE:_____

TODAY'S READING: Luke 13–15, Ecclesiastes 2

MY THOUGHTS:_____

_____

_____

_____

_____

_____

_____

_____

_____

_____

_____

_____

_____

_____

DATE: _____

TODAY'S READING: Luke 16-18, Ecclesiastes 3

MY THOUGHTS: _____

_____

_____

_____

_____

_____

_____

_____

_____

_____

_____

_____

_____

DATE: _____

TODAY'S READING: Luke 19-21, Ecclesiastes 4

MY THOUGHTS: _____

_____

_____

_____

_____

_____

_____

_____

_____

_____

_____

_____

_____

DATE: _____

TODAY'S READING: Luke 22-24, Ecclesiastes 5

MY THOUGHTS: _____

_____

_____

_____

_____

_____

_____

_____

_____

_____

_____

_____

_____

_____

DATE: _____

TODAY'S READING: Amos 1-3, Ecclesiastes 6

MY THOUGHTS: _____

_____

_____

_____

_____

_____

_____

_____

_____

_____

_____

_____

_____

_____

DATE: _____

MY THOUGHTS ON THIS WEEK'S READINGS: _____

_____
_____
_____
_____
_____
_____
_____
_____
_____
_____
_____
_____
_____
_____

DATE: _____

TODAY'S READING: Amos 4-6, Ecclesiastes 7

MY THOUGHTS: _____

_____
_____
_____
_____
_____
_____
_____
_____
_____
_____
_____
_____
_____
_____

DATE: _____

TODAY'S READING: Amos 7-9, Ecclesiastes 8

MY THOUGHTS: _____

_____

_____

_____

_____

_____

_____

_____

_____

_____

_____

_____

DATE: _____

TODAY'S READING: 1 Chronicles 1-4, Ecclesiastes 9

MY THOUGHTS: _____

_____

_____

_____

_____

_____

_____

_____

_____

_____

_____

_____

DATE: _____

TODAY'S READING: 1 Chronicles 5-8, Ecclesiastes 10

MY THOUGHTS: _____

_____

_____

_____

_____

_____

_____

_____

_____

_____

_____

_____

_____

_____

_____

DATE: _____

TODAY'S READING: 1 Chronicles 9-11, Ecclesiastes 11

MY THOUGHTS: _____

_____

_____

_____

_____

_____

_____

_____

_____

_____

_____

_____

_____

_____

DATE: _____

TODAY'S READING: 1 Chronicles 12-14, Ecclesiastes 12

MY THOUGHTS: _____

_____

_____

_____

_____

_____

_____

_____

_____

_____

_____

_____

DATE: _____

MY THOUGHTS ON THIS WEEK'S READINGS: _____

_____

_____

_____

_____

_____

_____

_____

_____

_____

_____

_____

_____

_____

DATE: ———————————

TODAY'S READING: 1 Chronicles 15-17, Song of Songs 1

MY THOUGHTS: ———————————

———————————————————————
———————————————————————
———————————————————————
———————————————————————
———————————————————————
———————————————————————
———————————————————————
———————————————————————
———————————————————————
———————————————————————
———————————————————————
———————————————————————
———————————————————————
———————————————————————

DATE: ———————————

TODAY'S READING: 1 Chronicles 18-20, Song of Songs 2

MY THOUGHTS: ———————————

———————————————————————
———————————————————————
———————————————————————
———————————————————————
———————————————————————
———————————————————————
———————————————————————
———————————————————————
———————————————————————
———————————————————————
———————————————————————
———————————————————————
———————————————————————
———————————————————————

DATE:_____

TODAY'S READING: 1 Chronicles 21-23, Song of Songs 3

MY THOUGHTS:_____

_____

_____

_____

_____

_____

_____

_____

_____

_____

_____

_____

_____

DATE:_____

TODAY'S READING: 1 Chronicles 24-26, Song of Songs 4

MY THOUGHTS:_____

_____

_____

_____

_____

_____

_____

_____

_____

_____

_____

_____

_____

_____

DATE: _____

TODAY'S READING: 1 Chronicles 27-29, Song of Songs 5

MY THOUGHTS: _____

_____

_____

_____

_____

_____

_____

_____

_____

_____

_____

_____

_____

_____

DATE: _____

TODAY'S READING: Hosea 1-4, Song of Songs 6

MY THOUGHTS: _____

_____

_____

_____

_____

_____

_____

_____

_____

_____

_____

_____

_____

_____

DATE: _____

MY THOUGHTS ON THIS WEEK'S READINGS: _____

_____

_____

_____

_____

_____

_____

_____

_____

_____

_____

_____

_____

_____

DATE: _____

TODAY'S READING: Hosea 5–8, Song of Songs 7

MY THOUGHTS: _____

_____

_____

_____

_____

_____

_____

_____

_____

_____

_____

_____

_____

DATE: ———————————

TODAY'S READING: Hosea 9-11, Song of Songs 8

MY THOUGHTS: ———————————————————————

———————————————————————————————

———————————————————————————————

———————————————————————————————

———————————————————————————————

———————————————————————————————

———————————————————————————————

———————————————————————————————

———————————————————————————————

———————————————————————————————

———————————————————————————————

———————————————————————————————

———————————————————————————————

———————————————————————————————

———————————————————————————————

DATE: ———————————

TODAY'S READING: Hosea 12-14, Psalm 95

MY THOUGHTS: ———————————————————————

———————————————————————————————

———————————————————————————————

———————————————————————————————

———————————————————————————————

———————————————————————————————

———————————————————————————————

———————————————————————————————

———————————————————————————————

———————————————————————————————

———————————————————————————————

———————————————————————————————

———————————————————————————————

DATE: _____

TODAY'S READING: 1 Corinthians 1-2, Psalm 96

MY THOUGHTS: _____

_____

_____

_____

_____

_____

_____

_____

_____

_____

_____

_____

_____

_____

DATE: _____

TODAY'S READING: 1 Corinthians 3-5, Psalm 97

MY THOUGHTS: _____

_____

_____

_____

_____

_____

_____

_____

_____

_____

_____

_____

_____

_____

DATE: _____

TODAY'S READING: 1 Corinthians 6–8, Psalm 98

MY THOUGHTS: _____

_____

_____

_____

_____

_____

_____

_____

_____

_____

_____

_____

_____

_____

DATE: _____

TODAY'S READING: 1 Corinthians 9-11, Psalm 99

MY THOUGHTS: _____

_____

_____

_____

_____

_____

_____

_____

_____

_____

_____

_____

_____

_____

DOERS OF THE WORD
by Sue Kline

"Be doers of the word, and not hearers only," warned James (Jas. 1:22, *NKJV*). Those who hear without doing, he continued, deceive themselves. Such self-deception can be a danger for believers. We congratulate ourselves for the number of Bible study guides we've completed. We're proud of how many times we've read the New Testament from beginning to end. But are we becoming doers of the Word?

I once remarked to a spiritual mentor, "Wow! I was really challenged by that message." Her response: "Yes, but were you changed?" Our heart cry when we encounter the words of the living God should be, "Lord, change me!"

Several years ago, I memorized Ps. 119:57-60, for it summarizes the way I want to respond to God's Word.

Determination: "You are my portion, O LORD; I have promised to obey your words."

Dependence: "I have sought your face with all my heart; be gracious to me according to your promise."

Deliberation: "I have considered my ways and have turned my steps to your statutes."

Decision: "I will hasten and not delay to obey your commands."

Adopt these attitudes of the psalmist and you will become a mighty doer of the Word.

—Adapted from "Doers of the Word" (Discipleship Journal, *Issue 98*).

Therefore,
if anyone
is in Christ,
he is a new
creation; the old
is gone, the
new has come!

2 Cor. 5:17

MONTH 8

DATE:_____

TODAY'S READING: 1 Corinthians 12-14, Psalm 100

MY THOUGHTS:_____

_____

_____

_____

_____

_____

_____

_____

_____

_____

_____

_____

_____

_____

DATE:_____

TODAY'S READING: 1 Corinthians 15-16, Psalm 101

MY THOUGHTS:_____

_____

_____

_____

_____

_____

_____

_____

_____

_____

_____

_____

_____

_____

DATE: ―――――――――――

TODAY'S READING: 2 Chronicles 1-4, Psalm 102

MY THOUGHTS: ――――――――――――――――――――

―――――――――――――――――――――――――――――――

―――――――――――――――――――――――――――――――

―――――――――――――――――――――――――――――――

―――――――――――――――――――――――――――――――

―――――――――――――――――――――――――――――――

―――――――――――――――――――――――――――――――

―――――――――――――――――――――――――――――――

―――――――――――――――――――――――――――――――

―――――――――――――――――――――――――――――――

―――――――――――――――――――――――――――――――

―――――――――――――――――――――――――――――――

―――――――――――――――――――――――――――――――

DATE: ―――――――――――

TODAY'S READING: 2 Chronicles 5-7, Psalm 103

MY THOUGHTS: ――――――――――――――――――――

―――――――――――――――――――――――――――――――

―――――――――――――――――――――――――――――――

―――――――――――――――――――――――――――――――

―――――――――――――――――――――――――――――――

―――――――――――――――――――――――――――――――

―――――――――――――――――――――――――――――――

―――――――――――――――――――――――――――――――

―――――――――――――――――――――――――――――――

―――――――――――――――――――――――――――――――

―――――――――――――――――――――――――――――――

―――――――――――――――――――――――――――――――

―――――――――――――――――――――――――――――――

DATE:_____

TODAY'S READING: 2 Chronicles 8-11, Psalm 104:1-23

MY THOUGHTS:_____

_____

_____

_____

_____

_____

_____

_____

_____

_____

_____

_____

_____

DATE:_____

TODAY'S READING: 2 Chronicles 12-15, Psalm 104:24-35

MY THOUGHTS:_____

_____

_____

_____

_____

_____

_____

_____

_____

_____

_____

_____

_____

DATE: _____

MY THOUGHTS ON THIS WEEK'S READINGS: _____

_____

_____

_____

_____

_____

_____

_____

_____

_____

_____

_____

_____

DATE: _____

TODAY'S READING: 2 Chronicles 16–18, Psalm 105

MY THOUGHTS: _____

_____

_____

_____

_____

_____

_____

_____

_____

_____

_____

_____

DATE:_____

TODAY'S READING: 2 Chronicles 19-21, Psalm 106:1-23

MY THOUGHTS:_____

_____

_____

_____

_____

_____

_____

_____

_____

_____

_____

_____

_____

DATE:_____

TODAY'S READING: 2 Chronicles 22-24, Psalm 106:24-48

MY THOUGHTS:_____

_____

_____

_____

_____

_____

_____

_____

_____

_____

_____

_____

_____

DATE: _____

TODAY'S READING: 2 Chronicles 25–27, Psalm 107

MY THOUGHTS: _____

_____

_____

_____

_____

_____

_____

_____

_____

_____

_____

_____

_____

_____

DATE: _____

TODAY'S READING: 2 Chronicles 28–30, Psalm 108

MY THOUGHTS: _____

_____

_____

_____

_____

_____

_____

_____

_____

_____

_____

_____

_____

DATE:_____

TODAY'S READING: 2 Chronicles 31–33, Psalm 109

MY THOUGHTS:_____

_____

_____

_____

_____

_____

_____

_____

_____

_____

_____

_____

_____

DATE:_____

MY THOUGHTS ON THIS WEEK'S READINGS:_____

_____

_____

_____

_____

_____

_____

_____

_____

_____

_____

_____

_____

_____

DATE: ————————————

TODAY'S READING: 2 Chronicles 34-36, Psalm 110

MY THOUGHTS: ————————————

_____

_____

_____

_____

_____

_____

_____

_____

_____

_____

_____

_____

_____

DATE: ————————————

TODAY'S READING: Obadiah, Psalm 111

MY THOUGHTS: ————————————

_____

_____

_____

_____

_____

_____

_____

_____

_____

_____

_____

_____

_____

DATE: _____

TODAY'S READING: 2 Corinthians 1-3, Psalm 112

MY THOUGHTS: _____

_____

_____

_____

_____

_____

_____

_____

_____

_____

_____

_____

_____

_____

DATE: _____

TODAY'S READING: 2 Corinthians 4-6, Psalm 113

MY THOUGHTS: _____

_____

_____

_____

_____

_____

_____

_____

_____

_____

_____

_____

_____

_____

DATE: _____

TODAY'S READING: 2 Corinthians 7-9, Psalm 114

MY THOUGHTS: _____

_____

_____

_____

_____

_____

_____

_____

_____

_____

_____

_____

_____

DATE: _____

TODAY'S READING: 2 Corinthians 10-13, Psalm 115

MY THOUGHTS: _____

_____

_____

_____

_____

_____

_____

_____

_____

_____

_____

_____

_____

DATE:_____

MY THOUGHTS ON THIS WEEK'S READINGS:_____

_____

_____

_____

_____

_____

_____

_____

_____

_____

_____

_____

_____

_____

_____

DATE:_____

TODAY'S READING: Ezra 1-4, Psalm 116

MY THOUGHTS:_____

_____

_____

_____

_____

_____

_____

_____

_____

_____

_____

_____

_____

_____

DATE: _____

TODAY'S READING: Ezra 5-7, Psalm 117

MY THOUGHTS: _____

_____

_____

_____

_____

_____

_____

_____

_____

_____

_____

_____

_____

DATE: _____

TODAY'S READING: Ezra 8-10, Psalm 118:1-14

MY THOUGHTS: _____

_____

_____

_____

_____

_____

_____

_____

_____

_____

_____

_____

_____

DATE:_____

TODAY'S READING: Nehemiah 1-3, Psalm 118:15-29

MY THOUGHTS:_____

_____

_____

_____

_____

_____

_____

_____

_____

_____

_____

_____

_____

_____

_____

DATE:_____

TODAY'S READING: Nehemiah 4-7, Psalm 119:1-16

MY THOUGHTS:_____

_____

_____

_____

_____

_____

_____

_____

_____

_____

_____

_____

_____

_____

_____

DATE: _____

TODAY'S READING: Nehemiah 8-10, Psalm 119:17-32

MY THOUGHTS: _____

_____

_____

_____

_____

_____

_____

_____

_____

_____

_____

_____

_____

_____

DATE: _____

TODAY'S READING: Nehemiah 11-13, Psalm 119:33-48

MY THOUGHTS: _____

_____

_____

_____

_____

_____

_____

_____

_____

_____

_____

_____

_____

_____

EMBEDDED TRUTH
by Jan Johnson

Consider how often we pick up ideas from those we spend time with—perhaps even their accent or odd laugh. Similarly, when we hear God speak to us in Scripture, the words and ideas percolate in our minds until we think they're our ideas. God rubs off on us, so to speak. We set out only to interact with God and enjoy God's presence, but we find to our surprise that we have soaked up the mind of Christ.

Authors Glandion Carney and William Long had this process in mind when they wrote about the purpose and place of Scripture in our lives:

> The heart of ethical mastery of the Scripture is to allow Scripture to move us. It is when Scripture becomes so deeply embedded in our lives that it need not be "drawn out" and "thought about" to have an influence. It becomes part of our very soul. It shapes us. Its very contours become the contours of our thoughts, words and hopes. This is beyond the stage where Scripture is used to extract comforting verses or even "principles of living." Scripture becomes our most engaging conversation partner.

When the Scriptures saturate our souls, we are more likely to act on them. This is different from articulating correct doctrine or professing profound ideas. Instead, truth becomes so deeply embedded in how we think and act that to act apart from it sounds ridiculous.

—Excerpted from "His Word, Your Words" (Discipleship Journal, *Issue 137).*

All Scripture is
God-breathed
and is useful
for teaching,
rebuking,
correcting and
training in
righteousness.

2 Tim. 3:16

MONTH 9

DATE: _____

TODAY'S READING: 1 Timothy 1-3, Psalm 119:49-64

MY THOUGHTS: _____

_____

_____

_____

_____

_____

_____

_____

_____

_____

_____

_____

_____

DATE: _____

TODAY'S READING: 1 Timothy 4-6, Psalm 119:65-80

MY THOUGHTS: _____

_____

_____

_____

_____

_____

_____

_____

_____

_____

_____

_____

_____

DATE: —————————————————

TODAY'S READING: Esther 1-3, Psalm 119:81-96

MY THOUGHTS: ———————————————————————

_____

_____

_____

_____

_____

_____

_____

_____

_____

_____

_____

_____

_____

DATE: —————————————————

TODAY'S READING: Esther 4-7, Psalm 119:97-112

MY THOUGHTS: ———————————————————————

_____

_____

_____

_____

_____

_____

_____

_____

_____

_____

_____

_____

DATE:_____

TODAY'S READING: Esther 8–10, Psalm 119:113–128

MY THOUGHTS:_____

_____

_____

_____

_____

_____

_____

_____

_____

_____

_____

_____

_____

_____

DATE:_____

TODAY'S READING: 2 Timothy, Psalm 119:129–144

MY THOUGHTS:_____

_____

_____

_____

_____

_____

_____

_____

_____

_____

_____

_____

_____

_____

DATE: _____

MY THOUGHTS ON THIS WEEK'S READINGS: _____

_____
_____
_____
_____
_____
_____
_____
_____
_____
_____
_____
_____
_____
_____

DATE: _____

TODAY'S READING: Job 1-3, Psalm 119:145-160

MY THOUGHTS: _____

_____
_____
_____
_____
_____
_____
_____
_____
_____
_____
_____
_____
_____

DATE: _____

TODAY'S READING: Job 4-6, Psalm 119:161-176

MY THOUGHTS: _____

_____

_____

_____

_____

_____

_____

_____

_____

_____

_____

_____

_____

_____

DATE: _____

TODAY'S READING: Job 7-9, Psalm 120

MY THOUGHTS: _____

_____

_____

_____

_____

_____

_____

_____

_____

_____

_____

_____

_____

DATE: _____

TODAY'S READING: Job 10-12, Psalm 121

MY THOUGHTS: _____

_____

_____

_____

_____

_____

_____

_____

_____

_____

_____

_____

_____

_____

_____

DATE: _____

TODAY'S READING: Job 13-15, Psalm 122

MY THOUGHTS: _____

_____

_____

_____

_____

_____

_____

_____

_____

_____

_____

_____

_____

_____

_____

DATE: _____

TODAY'S READING: Job 16-18, Isaiah 1

MY THOUGHTS: _____

_____

_____

_____

_____

_____

_____

_____

_____

_____

_____

_____

_____

DATE: _____

MY THOUGHTS ON THIS WEEK'S READINGS: _____

_____

_____

_____

_____

_____

_____

_____

_____

_____

_____

_____

_____

_____

DATE: _____

TODAY'S READING: Job 19-21, Isaiah 2

MY THOUGHTS: _____

_____

_____

_____

_____

_____

_____

_____

_____

_____

_____

_____

_____

_____

_____

DATE: _____

TODAY'S READING: Job 22-24, Isaiah 3

MY THOUGHTS: _____

_____

_____

_____

_____

_____

_____

_____

_____

_____

_____

_____

_____

_____

DATE:_____

TODAY'S READING: Job 25–27, Isaiah 4

MY THOUGHTS:_____

_____

_____

_____

_____

_____

_____

_____

_____

_____

_____

_____

_____

DATE:_____

TODAY'S READING: Job 28–30, Isaiah 5

MY THOUGHTS:_____

_____

_____

_____

_____

_____

_____

_____

_____

_____

_____

_____

_____

DATE: _____

TODAY'S READING: Job 31–33, Isaiah 6

MY THOUGHTS: _____

_____

_____

_____

_____

_____

_____

_____

_____

_____

_____

_____

_____

DATE: _____

TODAY'S READING: Job 34–36, Isaiah 7

MY THOUGHTS: _____

_____

_____

_____

_____

_____

_____

_____

_____

_____

_____

_____

_____

DATE: _____

MY THOUGHTS ON THIS WEEK'S READINGS: _____

_____

_____

_____

_____

_____

_____

_____

_____

_____

_____

_____

_____

_____

_____

DATE: _____

TODAY'S READING: Job 37–39, Isaiah 8

MY THOUGHTS: _____

_____

_____

_____

_____

_____

_____

_____

_____

_____

_____

_____

_____

DATE: ————————————

TODAY'S READING: Job 40–42, Isaiah 9

MY THOUGHTS: ————————————————————————

_____

_____

_____

_____

_____

_____

_____

_____

_____

_____

_____

_____

_____

DATE: ————————————

TODAY'S READING: Titus, Isaiah 10

MY THOUGHTS: ————————————————————————

_____

_____

_____

_____

_____

_____

_____

_____

_____

_____

_____

_____

DATE: _____

TODAY'S READING: Jeremiah 1-3, Isaiah 11

MY THOUGHTS: _____

_____

_____

_____

_____

_____

_____

_____

_____

_____

_____

_____

_____

DATE: _____

TODAY'S READING: Jeremiah 4-6, Isaiah 12

MY THOUGHTS: _____

_____

_____

_____

_____

_____

_____

_____

_____

_____

_____

_____

_____

_____

DATE: _____

TODAY'S READING: Jeremiah 7-9, Isaiah 13

MY THOUGHTS: _____

_____

_____

_____

_____

_____

_____

_____

_____

_____

_____

_____

_____

_____

DATE: _____

TODAY'S READING: Jeremiah 10-12, Isaiah 14

MY THOUGHTS: _____

_____

_____

_____

_____

_____

_____

_____

_____

_____

_____

_____

_____

Child of God, would you become a man [or woman] of God, strong in faith, full of blessing, rich in fruit to the glory of God? Be full of the Word of God, then; like Christ, make the Word your bread. Let it dwell richly in you. Have your heart full of it. Feed on it. Believe it. Obey it. It is only by believing and obeying that the Word can enter into our inward parts, into our very being.

Take it day by day as the Word that proceedeth—not has proceeded, but proceedeth, is proceeding—out of the mouth of God, as the Word of the living God, who in it holds living fellowship with His children, and speaks to them in living power. Take your thoughts of God's will, and God's work, and God's purpose with you and the world, not from the Church, not from Christians around you, but from the Word taught you by the Father; and, like Christ, you will be able to fulfill all that is written in the Scriptures concerning you.

—*Andrew Murray, excerpted from "Not by Bread Alone"*
(Discipleship Journal, Issue 64). Reprinted from
The Best of Andrew Murray by permission of Fleming H. Revell Co.

How great is
the love the
Father has
lavished on us,
that we should
be called
children of God!
And that is
what we are!

1 Jn. 3:1

MONTH 10

DATE:_____

TODAY'S READING: Jeremiah 13-15, Isaiah 15

MY THOUGHTS:_____

_____

_____

_____

_____

_____

_____

_____

_____

_____

_____

_____

_____

_____

DATE:_____

TODAY'S READING: Jeremiah 16-18, Isaiah 16

MY THOUGHTS:_____

_____

_____

_____

_____

_____

_____

_____

_____

_____

_____

_____

_____

_____

DATE: _____

TODAY'S READING: Jeremiah 19–21, Isaiah 17

MY THOUGHTS: _____

_____

_____

_____

_____

_____

_____

_____

_____

_____

_____

_____

_____

DATE: _____

TODAY'S READING: Jeremiah 22–24, Isaiah 18

MY THOUGHTS: _____

_____

_____

_____

_____

_____

_____

_____

_____

_____

_____

_____

_____

DATE: _____

TODAY'S READING: Jeremiah 25-27, Isaiah 19

MY THOUGHTS: _____

_____
_____
_____
_____
_____
_____
_____
_____
_____
_____
_____
_____

DATE: _____

TODAY'S READING: Jeremiah 28-30, Isaiah 20

MY THOUGHTS: _____

_____
_____
_____
_____
_____
_____
_____
_____
_____
_____
_____
_____

DATE: _____

MY THOUGHTS ON THIS WEEK'S READINGS: _____

_____

_____

_____

_____

_____

_____

_____

_____

_____

_____

_____

_____

_____

_____

DATE: _____

TODAY'S READING: Jeremiah 31-33, Isaiah 21

MY THOUGHTS: _____

_____

_____

_____

_____

_____

_____

_____

_____

_____

_____

_____

DATE: _____

TODAY'S READING: Jeremiah 34–36, Isaiah 22

MY THOUGHTS: _____

_____

_____

_____

_____

_____

_____

_____

_____

_____

_____

_____

_____

DATE: _____

TODAY'S READING: Jeremiah 37–39, Isaiah 23

MY THOUGHTS: _____

_____

_____

_____

_____

_____

_____

_____

_____

_____

_____

_____

_____

DATE: ―――――――――――――

TODAY'S READING: Jeremiah 40-42, Isaiah 24

MY THOUGHTS: ―――――――――――――――――――――――――――――――

―――

―――

―――

―――

―――

―――

―――

―――

―――

―――

―――

―――

―――

DATE: ―――――――――――――

TODAY'S READING: Jeremiah 43-46, Isaiah 25

MY THOUGHTS: ―――――――――――――――――――――――――――――――

―――

―――

―――

―――

―――

―――

―――

―――

―――

―――

―――

―――

DATE:_____

TODAY'S READING: Jeremiah 47–49, Isaiah 26

MY THOUGHTS:_____

_____

_____

_____

_____

_____

_____

_____

_____

_____

_____

_____

_____

_____

DATE:_____

MY THOUGHTS ON THIS WEEK'S READINGS:_____

_____

_____

_____

_____

_____

_____

_____

_____

_____

_____

_____

_____

_____

_____

DATE: _____

TODAY'S READING: Jeremiah 50-52, Isaiah 27

MY THOUGHTS: _____

_____

_____

_____

_____

_____

_____

_____

_____

_____

_____

_____

_____

DATE: _____

TODAY'S READING: Lamentations 1-2, Isaiah 28

MY THOUGHTS: _____

_____

_____

_____

_____

_____

_____

_____

_____

_____

_____

_____

_____

DATE: _____

TODAY'S READING: Lamentations 3-5, Isaiah 29

MY THOUGHTS: _____

_____

_____

_____

_____

_____

_____

_____

_____

_____

_____

_____

_____

DATE: _____

TODAY'S READING: 1 John 1-3, Isaiah 30

MY THOUGHTS: _____

_____

_____

_____

_____

_____

_____

_____

_____

_____

_____

_____

_____

DATE: _____

TODAY'S READING: 1 John 4-5, Isaiah 31

MY THOUGHTS: _____

_____

_____

_____

_____

_____

_____

_____

_____

_____

_____

_____

_____

_____

DATE: _____

TODAY'S READING: 2 & 3 John, Isaiah 32

MY THOUGHTS: _____

_____

_____

_____

_____

_____

_____

_____

_____

_____

_____

_____

_____

_____

DATE: _____

MY THOUGHTS ON THIS WEEK'S READINGS: _____

_____

_____

_____

_____

_____

_____

_____

_____

_____

_____

_____

_____

_____

DATE: _____

TODAY'S READING: 1 Peter 1–3, Isaiah 33

MY THOUGHTS: _____

_____

_____

_____

_____

_____

_____

_____

_____

_____

_____

_____

_____

DATE: ————————————

TODAY'S READING: 1 Peter 4-5, Isaiah 34

MY THOUGHTS: ————————————————————

_____

_____

_____

_____

_____

_____

_____

_____

_____

_____

_____

DATE: ————————————

TODAY'S READING: Ezekiel 1-4, Isaiah 35

MY THOUGHTS: ————————————————————

_____

_____

_____

_____

_____

_____

_____

_____

_____

_____

_____

DATE: _____

TODAY'S READING: Ezekiel 5-7, Isaiah 36

MY THOUGHTS: _____

_____

_____

_____

_____

_____

_____

_____

_____

_____

_____

_____

_____

_____

DATE: _____

TODAY'S READING: Ezekiel 8-11, Isaiah 37

MY THOUGHTS: _____

_____

_____

_____

_____

_____

_____

_____

_____

_____

_____

_____

_____

_____

DATE: _____

TODAY'S READING: Ezekiel 12-15, Isaiah 38

MY THOUGHTS: _____

_____

_____

_____

_____

_____

_____

_____

_____

_____

_____

_____

_____

DATE: _____

TODAY'S READING: Ezekiel 16-19, Isaiah 39

MY THOUGHTS: _____

_____

_____

_____

_____

_____

_____

_____

_____

_____

_____

_____

_____

EMPOWER YOUR PRAYERS
WITH SCRIPTURE
by Joni Eareckson Tada

I have learned to season my prayers with the Word of God. It's a way of talking to God in His language.

When we bring God's Word directly into our praying, we are bringing God's power into our praying. Hebrews 4:12 declares, "For the word of God is living and active. Sharper than any double-edged sword." God's Word is living, and so it infuses our prayers with life and vitality. God's Word is also active, injecting energy and power into our prayer.

I'm convinced that when we consciously employ God's Word in our prayers, it shows Him the importance we attach to our requests. It demonstrates we have thought through our petitions and praises and lined them up against the plumb line of Scripture. It underscores to Him the high regard and appreciation we attach to His Word and demonstrates that we sincerely seek His heart in the matter for which we pray. Using God's Word in prayer gives a divine familiarity to our words, earmarking us as servants who possess a working knowledge of the most powerful prayer book ever written: the Bible.

Saints in Scripture practiced this type of praying. The prophet Habakkuk appealed to God on the basis of His Word during a time of deep national distress. He quoted snippets of psalms and proverbs as he spoke with God: "Your eyes are too pure to look on evil; you cannot tolerate wrong. Why then do you tolerate the treacherous? Why are you silent while the wicked swallow up those more righteous than themselves?" (Hab. 1:13).

David pleaded with God in prayer based on what he knew to be true about the Lord from Scripture: "Remember, O Lord, your great mercy and love, for they are from of old. . . . According to your love remember me, for you are good, O Lord" (Ps. 25:6-7).

Does it sound cheeky to remind God of His character and His promises? Does it seem presumptuous? Perhaps, if you are unfamiliar with the prayer habits of saints such as Habakkuk and David. Nevertheless, the Lord would have us claim His love, plead His holiness, remind Him of His goodness, recount His longsuffering, present to Him His steadfastness, and pray in His power. In Is. 1:18, God invites us: "Come now, let us reason together." He encourages our discourse.

—*Excerpted from "Speaking God's Language" (*Discipleship Journal, *Issue 111).*

The grass

withers and

the flowers fall,

but the word

of our God

stands forever.

Is. 40:8

MONTH 11

DATE: _____

TODAY'S READING: Ezekiel 20-23, Psalm 123-124

MY THOUGHTS: _____

_____

_____

_____

_____

_____

_____

_____

_____

_____

_____

_____

_____

DATE: _____

TODAY'S READING: Ezekiel 24-26, Psalm 125-126

MY THOUGHTS: _____

_____

_____

_____

_____

_____

_____

_____

_____

_____

_____

_____

_____

DATE: —————————————————

TODAY'S READING: Ezekiel 27-30, Psalm 127

MY THOUGHTS: ————————————————————————————————

_____

_____

_____

_____

_____

_____

_____

_____

_____

_____

_____

_____

_____

DATE: —————————————————

TODAY'S READING: Ezekiel 31-34, Psalm 128-129

MY THOUGHTS: ————————————————————————————————

_____

_____

_____

_____

_____

_____

_____

_____

_____

_____

_____

_____

DATE: _____

TODAY'S READING: Ezekiel 35-38, Psalm 130-131

MY THOUGHTS: _____

_____

_____

_____

_____

_____

_____

_____

_____

_____

_____

_____

_____

DATE: _____

TODAY'S READING: Ezekiel 39-42, Psalm 132

MY THOUGHTS: _____

_____

_____

_____

_____

_____

_____

_____

_____

_____

_____

_____

DATE: _____

MY THOUGHTS ON THIS WEEK'S READINGS: _____

_____
_____
_____
_____
_____
_____
_____
_____
_____
_____
_____
_____
_____
_____
_____
_____

DATE: _____

TODAY'S READING: Ezekiel 43-45, Psalm 133-134

MY THOUGHTS: _____

_____
_____
_____
_____
_____
_____
_____
_____
_____
_____
_____
_____
_____
_____

DATE: _____

TODAY'S READING: Ezekiel 46–48, Psalm 135

MY THOUGHTS: _____

_____

_____

_____

_____

_____

_____

_____

_____

_____

_____

_____

_____

DATE: _____

TODAY'S READING: John 1–3, Psalm 136

MY THOUGHTS: _____

_____

_____

_____

_____

_____

_____

_____

_____

_____

_____

_____

_____

DATE: _____

TODAY'S READING: John 4-6, Psalm 137

MY THOUGHTS: _____

_____

_____

_____

_____

_____

_____

_____

_____

_____

_____

_____

_____

DATE: _____

TODAY'S READING: John 7-9, Psalm 138

MY THOUGHTS: _____

_____

_____

_____

_____

_____

_____

_____

_____

_____

_____

_____

DATE: _____

TODAY'S READING: John 10-12, Psalm 139

MY THOUGHTS: _____

_____

_____

_____

_____

_____

_____

_____

_____

_____

_____

_____

DATE: _____

MY THOUGHTS ON THIS WEEK'S READINGS: _____

_____

_____

_____

_____

_____

_____

_____

_____

_____

_____

_____

_____

DATE: _____
TODAY'S READING: John 13-15, Psalm 140
MY THOUGHTS: _____
_____
_____
_____
_____
_____
_____
_____
_____
_____
_____
_____
_____
_____

DATE: _____
TODAY'S READING: John 16-18, Psalm 141
MY THOUGHTS: _____
_____
_____
_____
_____
_____
_____
_____
_____
_____
_____
_____
_____

DATE: _____

TODAY'S READING: John 19-21, Psalm 142

MY THOUGHTS: _____

_____

_____

_____

_____

_____

_____

_____

_____

_____

_____

_____

_____

_____

DATE: _____

TODAY'S READING: Daniel 1-3, Psalm 143

MY THOUGHTS: _____

_____

_____

_____

_____

_____

_____

_____

_____

_____

_____

_____

_____

_____

DATE: ———————————————

TODAY'S READING: Daniel 4-6, Psalm 144

MY THOUGHTS: ————————————————————

———————————————————————————————

———————————————————————————————

———————————————————————————————

———————————————————————————————

———————————————————————————————

———————————————————————————————

———————————————————————————————

———————————————————————————————

———————————————————————————————

———————————————————————————————

———————————————————————————————

———————————————————————————————

DATE: ———————————————

TODAY'S READING: Daniel 7-9, Psalm 145

MY THOUGHTS: ————————————————————

———————————————————————————————

———————————————————————————————

———————————————————————————————

———————————————————————————————

———————————————————————————————

———————————————————————————————

———————————————————————————————

———————————————————————————————

———————————————————————————————

———————————————————————————————

———————————————————————————————

———————————————————————————————

DATE: _____

MY THOUGHTS ON THIS WEEK'S READINGS: _____

_____

_____

_____

_____

_____

_____

_____

_____

_____

_____

_____

_____

_____

_____

DATE: _____

TODAY'S READING: Daniel 10-12, Psalm 146

MY THOUGHTS: _____

_____

_____

_____

_____

_____

_____

_____

_____

_____

_____

_____

_____

_____

DATE: _____

TODAY'S READING: 1 Thessalonians 1-2, Psalm 147

MY THOUGHTS: _____

_____

_____

_____

_____

_____

_____

_____

_____

_____

_____

_____

_____

_____

DATE: _____

TODAY'S READING: 1 Thessalonians 3-5, Psalm 148

MY THOUGHTS: _____

_____

_____

_____

_____

_____

_____

_____

_____

_____

_____

_____

_____

_____

DATE: _____

TODAY'S READING: Joel, Psalm 149

MY THOUGHTS: _____

_____

_____

_____

_____

_____

_____

_____

_____

_____

_____

_____

_____

DATE: _____

TODAY'S READING: Micah 1–3, Psalm 150

MY THOUGHTS: _____

_____

_____

_____

_____

_____

_____

_____

_____

_____

_____

_____

_____

DATE: _____

TODAY'S READING: Micah 4-5, Isaiah 40

MY THOUGHTS: _____

_____

_____

_____

_____

_____

_____

_____

_____

_____

_____

_____

_____

_____

DATE: _____

TODAY'S READING: Micah 6-7, Isaiah 41

MY THOUGHTS: _____

_____

_____

_____

_____

_____

_____

_____

_____

_____

_____

_____

_____

A CONTRITE SPIRIT

by Jean Fleming

If I were to choose one verse to capsulate the essential attitudes I believe God looks for in His people as they approach His Word, Is. 66:2 would get my vote: "This is the one I esteem: he who is humble and contrite in spirit, and trembles at my word." We don't hear much about sticking a humble and contrite spirit and a good solid tremble in with our Bible study helps, but without them we will always shuffle around the edges and never penetrate to the heart of God's riches.

The Word comes in love to bruise as well as to bless. If we come to the Word as self-sufficient, self-satisfied consumers of blessing, the blessing cannot penetrate the armor of self. The Word of God must pierce our thick skins, must strike stinging blows at times, must put our hips out of joint, must hold a mirror before our faces that we might see what our sin is doing to us. The Word must wound before it binds up. Otherwise, far worse sores fester out of sight, waiting to erupt and destroy us. A contrite spirit welcomes God's work that reveals who we really are. It limps to the throne of grace to receive the healing balm.

*—Excerpted from "Open-Heart Bible Study" (*Discipleship Journal, *Issue 89).*

May our
Lord Jesus Christ
himself and
God our
Father . . .
encourage your
hearts and
strengthen you
in every good
deed and word.

2 Thess. 2:16-17

MONTH 12

DATE:_____

TODAY'S READING: 2 Thessalonians, Isaiah 42

MY THOUGHTS:_____

_____

_____

_____

_____

_____

_____

_____

_____

_____

_____

_____

_____

_____

DATE:_____

TODAY'S READING: Nahum, Isaiah 43

MY THOUGHTS:_____

_____

_____

_____

_____

_____

_____

_____

_____

_____

_____

_____

_____

_____

DATE: _____

TODAY'S READING: 2 Peter, Isaiah 44

MY THOUGHTS: _____

_____

_____

_____

_____

_____

_____

_____

_____

_____

_____

_____

_____

_____

DATE: _____

TODAY'S READING: Habakkuk, Isaiah 45

MY THOUGHTS: _____

_____

_____

_____

_____

_____

_____

_____

_____

_____

_____

_____

_____

_____

DATE: _____

TODAY'S READING: Zephaniah, Isaiah 46

MY THOUGHTS: _____

_____

_____

_____

_____

_____

_____

_____

_____

_____

_____

_____

_____

_____

DATE: _____

TODAY'S READING: Jude, Isaiah 47

MY THOUGHTS: _____

_____

_____

_____

_____

_____

_____

_____

_____

_____

_____

_____

_____

DATE: _____

MY THOUGHTS ON THIS WEEK'S READINGS: _____

_____

_____

_____

_____

_____

_____

_____

_____

_____

_____

_____

_____

_____

DATE: _____

TODAY'S READING: Haggai, Isaiah 48

MY THOUGHTS: _____

_____

_____

_____

_____

_____

_____

_____

_____

_____

_____

_____

_____

DATE: _____

TODAY'S READING: Zechariah 1–3, Isaiah 49

MY THOUGHTS: _____

_____

_____

_____

_____

_____

_____

_____

_____

_____

_____

_____

_____

_____

DATE: _____

TODAY'S READING: Zechariah 4–6, Isaiah 50

MY THOUGHTS: _____

_____

_____

_____

_____

_____

_____

_____

_____

_____

_____

_____

_____

_____

DATE: ————————————

TODAY'S READING: Zechariah 7-9, Isaiah 51

MY THOUGHTS: ————————————————————————

———————————————————————————————————————

———————————————————————————————————————

———————————————————————————————————————

———————————————————————————————————————

———————————————————————————————————————

———————————————————————————————————————

———————————————————————————————————————

———————————————————————————————————————

———————————————————————————————————————

———————————————————————————————————————

———————————————————————————————————————

———————————————————————————————————————

DATE: ————————————

TODAY'S READING: Zechariah 10-12, Isaiah 52

MY THOUGHTS: ————————————————————————

———————————————————————————————————————

———————————————————————————————————————

———————————————————————————————————————

———————————————————————————————————————

———————————————————————————————————————

———————————————————————————————————————

———————————————————————————————————————

———————————————————————————————————————

———————————————————————————————————————

———————————————————————————————————————

———————————————————————————————————————

DATE: _____

TODAY'S READING: Zechariah 13-14, Isaiah 53

MY THOUGHTS: _____

_____

_____

_____

_____

_____

_____

_____

_____

_____

_____

_____

_____

DATE: _____

MY THOUGHTS ON THIS WEEK'S READINGS: _____

_____

_____

_____

_____

_____

_____

_____

_____

_____

_____

_____

_____

_____

DATE: —————————————

TODAY'S READING: Malachi 1-2, Isaiah 54

MY THOUGHTS: ——————————————————————————

_____

_____

_____

_____

_____

_____

_____

_____

_____

_____

_____

_____

_____

DATE: —————————————

TODAY'S READING: Malachi 3-4, Isaiah 55

MY THOUGHTS: ——————————————————————————

_____

_____

_____

_____

_____

_____

_____

_____

_____

_____

_____

_____

_____

DATE: _____

TODAY'S READING: Revelation 1-2, Isaiah 56

MY THOUGHTS: _____

_____

_____

_____

_____

_____

_____

_____

_____

_____

_____

_____

_____

DATE: _____

TODAY'S READING: Revelation 3-4, Isaiah 57

MY THOUGHTS: _____

_____

_____

_____

_____

_____

_____

_____

_____

_____

_____

_____

_____

DATE: —————————————

TODAY'S READING: Revelation 5-6, Isaiah 58

MY THOUGHTS: —————————————————————

———————————————————————————————————

———————————————————————————————————

———————————————————————————————————

———————————————————————————————————

———————————————————————————————————

———————————————————————————————————

———————————————————————————————————

———————————————————————————————————

———————————————————————————————————

———————————————————————————————————

———————————————————————————————————

———————————————————————————————————

DATE: —————————————

TODAY'S READING: Revelation 7-8, Isaiah 59

MY THOUGHTS: —————————————————————

———————————————————————————————————

———————————————————————————————————

———————————————————————————————————

———————————————————————————————————

———————————————————————————————————

———————————————————————————————————

———————————————————————————————————

———————————————————————————————————

———————————————————————————————————

———————————————————————————————————

———————————————————————————————————

———————————————————————————————————

DATE: _____

MY THOUGHTS ON THIS WEEK'S READINGS: _____

_____

_____

_____

_____

_____

_____

_____

_____

_____

_____

_____

_____

_____

DATE: _____

TODAY'S READING: Revelation 9-10, Isaiah 60

MY THOUGHTS: _____

_____

_____

_____

_____

_____

_____

_____

_____

_____

_____

_____

_____

DATE: —————————————

TODAY'S READING: Revelation 11-12, Isaiah 61

MY THOUGHTS: ————————————————————————

_____

_____

_____

_____

_____

_____

_____

_____

_____

_____

_____

_____

DATE: —————————————

TODAY'S READING: Revelation 13-14, Isaiah 62

MY THOUGHTS: ————————————————————————

_____

_____

_____

_____

_____

_____

_____

_____

_____

_____

_____

_____

BIBLE READING JOURNAL

DATE: _____

TODAY'S READING: Revelation 15–16, Isaiah 63

MY THOUGHTS: _____

_____

_____

_____

_____

_____

_____

_____

_____

_____

_____

_____

DATE: _____

TODAY'S READING: Revelation 17–18, Isaiah 64

MY THOUGHTS: _____

_____

_____

_____

_____

_____

_____

_____

_____

_____

_____

_____

DATE: —————————————

TODAY'S READING: Revelation 19-20, Isaiah 65

MY THOUGHTS: ——————————————————————————

_____

_____

_____

_____

_____

_____

_____

_____

_____

_____

_____

_____

DATE: —————————————

TODAY'S READING: Revelation 21-22, Isaiah 66

MY THOUGHTS: ——————————————————————————

_____

_____

_____

_____

_____

_____

_____

_____

_____

_____

_____

_____

A n old writer said that some books are to be tasted, some to be swallowed, some to be chewed and digested. The Bible is one that you can never finish with. It is like a bottomless well; you can always find fresh truth gushing forth from its pages. "No Scripture," said [Charles] Spurgeon, "is exhausted by a single explanation. The flowers of God's garden bloom not only double, but sevenfold; they are continually pouring forth fresh fragrance." Hence the great fascination of constant and earnest Bible study. I thank God there is a height in the Book that I have never been able to reach, a depth that I have never been able to fathom.

—*Dwight L. Moody,* Golden Counsels

LOOKING FOR YOUR NEXT BIBLE STUDY

Beating Busyness
by Adam Holz • 978-1-57683-155-7

Despite technological advances and enhanced communication, our "to do" lists are longer than ever. Identify and tackle stressful issues in your life through articles, questions, quotes, Scripture, and related exercises. Based on excerpts from top *Discipleship Journal* articles, this study will challenge you to deal effectively with busyness.

Building Better Relationships
by Susan Nikaido • 978-1-57683-167-0

Based on top *Discipleship Journal* articles, this Bible study offers a wealth of insight to help you develop deeper vulnerability, sensitivity, and love in all your relationships—at work, home, or anywhere.

Growing Deeper with God
by Susan Nikaido • 978-1-57683-153-3

Discover how you can become an intimate friend of God. Learn to focus on Him and reorder your priorities as you interact with God personally. Begin to experience the kind of closeness with God that your heart longs for.

Redeeming Failure
by Michael M. Smith • 978-1-57683-164-9

Does failure frighten you? Get beyond its paralyzing effects and learn how failure can be a necessary discipline to grow in Christ. For growing or mature believers, this *Discipleship Journal* Bible study is designed to help you develop a deeper relationship with God.

To get your copies, visit your local bookstore, call **1-800-366-7788**, or go to **www.discipleshipjournal.com** or **www.navpress.com**.

TRY ONE OF THESE GREAT STUDIES FROM

 Discipleship Journal.®

Becoming More Like Jesus
by Michael M. Smith • 978-1-57683-156-4

Becoming like Jesus is a process, not learning a list of rules. Based on excerpts from top *Discipleship Journal* articles, this study will develop His character in you as you evaluate your life, understand Jesus' teachings on character, and live them out.

Following God in Tough Times
by Michael M. Smith • 978-1-57683-157-1

Even when we feel imprisoned by life's difficult circumstances, God gives us freedom to choose how we'll respond. Learn how to accept and gain perspective on tough times as you move from survival to service.

Nurturing a Passion for Prayer
by Michael M. Smith • 978-1-57683-165-6

Is your experience with prayer less than passionate communication with God? Change your attitude toward prayer. The staff of *Discipleship Journal* designed this study to help you discover intimate interaction with the heavenly Father.

Your Money and Your Life
by Sue Kline • 978-1-57683-166-3

Discover how to handle your finances and your possessions—whether many or few—in a way that leaves you free to find true satisfaction, generosity, and contentment with what God has given you.